LIBRARY DISTRICT NO. 1
206 SOUTH BROADWAY
P.O. BOX 398
LOUISBURG, KS 66053

DEMCO

Showing Distance in art

Joy Richardson

Gareth Stevens Publishing
MILWAUKEE

For a free color catalog describing Gareth Stevens' list of high-quality books and multimedia programs, call 1-800-542-2595 (USA) or 1-800-461-9120 (Canada). Gareth Stevens Publishing's Fax: (414) 225-0377.

Gareth Stevens Publishing would like to thank Gundega Spons of the Milwaukee Art Museum for her kind and professional help with the information in this book.

Library of Congress Cataloging-in-Publication Data available upon request from publisher.
Fax (414) 225-0377 for the attention of the Publishing Records Department.

ISBN 0-8368-2627-2

This North American edition first published in 2000 by
Gareth Stevens Publishing
1555 North RiverCenter Drive, Suite 201
Milwaukee, Wisconsin 53212 USA

Original edition © 1997 by Franklin Watts. First published in 1997 as *In the Distance* by Franklin Watts, 96 Leonard Street, London, EC2A 4RH, United Kingdom. This U.S. edition © 2000 by Gareth Stevens, Inc. Additional end matter © 2000 by Gareth Stevens, Inc.

Gareth Stevens Editor: Monica Rausch
Gareth Stevens Cover Designer: Joel Bucaro
U.K. Editor: Sarah Ridley
U.K. Art Director: Robert Walster
U.K. Designer: Louise Thomas

Photographs: © photo RMN/Jean/Monet/La Rue Montorgueil pp. 22-23, van Gogh/The Bedroom pp. 24-25; reproduced by courtesy of the Trustees, The National Gallery, London Hobbema/The Avenue, Middleharnis pp. 14-15, 29 (detail); Uccello/The Battle of San Romano pp. 4-5; van der Weyden/St. Ivo pp. 6-7, 27 (details); Pinturicchio/Scenes from the Odyssey pp. 8-9, Brueghel/The Adoration of the Kings cover, pp. 10-11, 26 (detail), 28 (detail); Steenwyck/The Courtyard of a Renaissance Palace pp. 12-13, 30 (detail); Degas/Beach Scene pp. 20-21, 28 (detail); National Gallery of Scotland, Niagara Falls, Frederick Church pp. 18-19, 31 (detail); © Tate Gallery, London Constable/Flatford Mills pp. 16-17.

Printed in Mexico

1 2 3 4 5 6 7 8 9 04 03 02 01 00

Contents

For additional information about the artists and paintings, see pages 30-31.

The Rout of San Romano
painted by Paolo Uccello

Uccello painted this battle on a flat surface,
but he figured out how to show action
in the distance as well as close up.

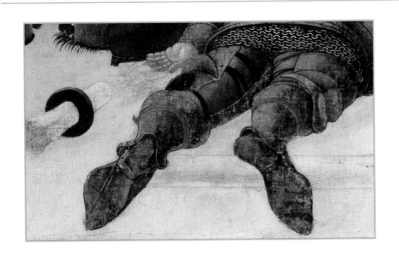

These feet look big as they stick out toward you.

Compare the size of the horses in the foreground with these horses galloping away.

Uccello makes faraway trees look smaller and paler.

St. Ivo
painted by Rogier van der Weyden

This painting makes your eye move
back and forth between the man and
the view outside his window.

The man fills the foreground, reading this writing.

Take a look through the window at life outside.

Follow the horse up the path to the castle.

Look how the faraway hills fade to a hazy blue.

Penelope with the Suitors
painted by Bernardino di Betto Pinturicchio

Penelope weaves and waits for Ulysses to come home from the wars. He has arrived at last.

Find all the lines that
lead toward the window.

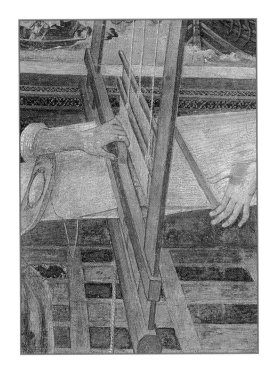

The hero's ship and
the distant sea help
tell the story.

Ulysses is in the background.
Has Penelope noticed him yet?

The Adoration of the Kings
painted by Jan Brueghel the Elder

People gather as the kings bring gifts to Jesus.

The rickety stable fills
half the picture.

You can see an
entire town in
the background.

People are everywhere.
How many can you count?

Faces at the back of the
crowd are smaller.

People grow
fainter in
the distance.

The Courtyard of
a Renaissance Palace
painted by Hendrick van Steenwyck

The painter lined up the buildings to
give a perfect view of this imaginary palace.

Follow the straight lines back into the painting. The lines lead your eyes to the far archway.

The pillars in the distance look smaller than those in front.

You can see up into this room.

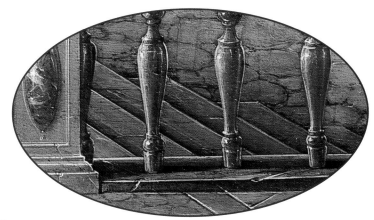

Look how light shapes the steps.

The Avenue, Middelharnis

painted by Meindert Hobbema

Hobbema liked the pattern of the trees
lining this road into town.

The road and trees make triangle
shapes pointing into the distance.

How far apart
are these people?

Sky meets Earth at
the low horizon.

Trees soar high
into the sky.

Flatford Mill
painted by John Constable

Constable knew every inch of this river as a child.
His eyes recorded it in his memory.

What is this horse pulling?

Walk your eyes along the path. Whom do you meet?

Glimpse the river again as it winds around the corner.

Look at the clouds stacked above the horizon.

Niagara Falls
painted by Frederick Edwin Church

Rushing, tumbling, spraying water fills the painting as far as the eye can see.

Look directly across to
the far bank of the river.

Watch the water
tumbling over the edge.

Other people are watching.
Tiny figures help show the
size of the waterfall.

Where does the rainbow start?

Beach Scene
painted by Edgar Degas

Degas painted the hair-combing scene indoors, in his studio, and then he filled in a beach background.

Look at the high horizon.
How much of the painting
is sea and sky?

Hands carefully comb
hair in the foreground.

Scattered objects
look large on
the sand.

Black blobs make distant bathers.

La Rue Montorgueil

painted by Claude Monet

On festival day in Paris, flags deck
the buildings. Crowds gather in the street.

Looking at this picture, you seem to be high up looking down and along the street. How far can you see?

The closest buildings look taller.

Flags are larger near the front of the picture.

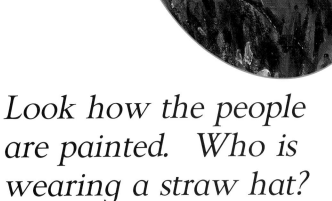

Look how the people are painted. Who is wearing a straw hat?

The Bedroom at Arles
painted by Vincent van Gogh

Van Gogh loved this simple room
in a house he had rented.

To make it look closer, one end of the bed is painted larger than the other.

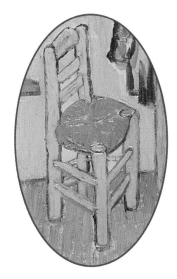

Which chair leg is closest to you?

Light changes the blue color of the walls where they meet.

Look how the table's square corners appear triangular.

Near and Far

Changing sizes

Objects that are close to you look big. Objects farther away look smaller.

Try drawing a person in the foreground with buildings or trees in the background. Use different sizes to show the distance between them.

For help, look back at pages 4, 10, and 16.

Through the window

Try making a "near-and-far" painting.

*Paint a wall with a window
or an open door and the view
you can see through it.*

For help, look back at pages 6 and 8.

Faraway colors

Have you noticed that colors in the
distance often look lighter and hazier?

*Mix colors carefully to paint
a picture with water, hills,
or buildings in the distance.*

For help, look at pages 4, 6, and 10.

On the horizon

The sky seems to come right down
to meet Earth at the horizon.

Look out of the window and paint the horizon you can see.
You can choose to place the horizon low or high in the painting.

For help, look at pages
14, 16, and 20.

Crowd control

Try painting lots of people in
a picture. Make the people
in front bigger and those in
back smaller. Distant people
need less detail.

For help, look
back at pages
10, 20, and 22.

Meeting points

If you look straight ahead along a road or a hallway,
the sides seem to move closer together in the distance.

*High lines, like the tops of
trees, seem to lead the eye
downward. Low lines,
like the edge of the road,
seem to lead the eye up
into the distance.*

*Look straight ahead along
a path or down a hallway.
Try drawing what you see,
showing lines leading into
the distance.*

For help, look at pages 14, 22, and 24.

More about the paintings in this book

■ The Rout of San Romano *(page 4)*

Paolo Uccello (1397-1475) lived in Florence. This painting, showing victory in a skirmish against Siena, was made to decorate the palace of the ruling Medici family. Uccello loved working with perspective, as seen in the fallen knight, the arrangement of lances on the ground, and even the size of the big red hat.

■ St. Ivo *(page 6)*

Rogier van der Weyden (about 1400-1464) was Flemish and was once the official painter for the city of Brussels. Saint Ivo was the patron saint of lawyers and defended the poor. In this painting, he is probably reading a legal document, while daily life goes on in the background.

■ Penelope with the Suitors *(page 8)*

Bernardino di Betto Pinturicchio (about 1454-1513) was Italian. He painted this picture on plaster to decorate a wall in the royal palace in Siena. It shows a scene from Homer's *Odyssey*. After ten years of wandering and adventures, Ulysses returned from the Trojan Wars and confronted the suitors who had been wooing his wife.

■ The Adoration of the Kings *(page 10)*

Jan Brueghel the Elder (1568-1625) belonged to a famous family of Flemish painters. His paintings are filled with details from his own time. This interesting scene shows kings, shepherds, a crowd of on-lookers, and an entire Flemish town in the background.

■ The Courtyard of a Renaissance Palace *(page 12)*

Hendrick van Steenwyck (about 1580-1649) was Flemish but lived in Frankfurt, London, and the Netherlands. He specialized in painting the architecture of buildings. This fantasy picture shows his skill in creating perspective. All the lines along steps, railings, and floor tiles seem to lead back to the same point in the distance, known as the *vanishing point*. The people were painted in afterward by someone else.

The Avenue, Middelharnis *(page 14)*

Meindert Hobbema (1638-1709) lived in Holland. He gave up professional painting when he was thirty to go into the wine business. Twenty years later, on a visit to southern Holland, he saw this avenue of tall, bare trees soaring into the sky and thought it would make a good painting. It became his most famous work.

Flatford Mill *(page 16)*

John Constable (1776-1837) grew up in Suffolk, England. His father owned the mill at Flatford on the River Stour, which appears in this painting. Constable drew inspiration for paintings from the familiar scenes of his childhood. He wanted to show nature truthfully in all its simple beauty.

Niagara Falls *(page 18)*

Frederick Edwin Church (1826-1900) was an American landscape painter. He liked painting nature in the dramatic, breathtaking forms of waterfalls, rainbows, storms, and icebergs. This painting shows the Niagara Falls from the American side with Canada across the river.

Beach Scene *(page 20)*

Edgar Degas (1834-1917) was one of a group of French painters who became known as impressionists. Like some of his friends, he preferred painting indoors. He posed the nursemaid combing the girl's hair in his studio. He painted the golden beach to make a good background.

La Rue Montorgueil *(page 22)*

Of all the French impressionists, Claude Monet (1840-1926) was the one who was best known for his exploration of the effects of light and color, as seen in this painting. The painting captures the joyfulness of a holiday celebrating the Universal Exhibition in Paris in 1878.

The Bedroom at Arles *(page 24)*

Vincent van Gogh (1853-90) rented the "Yellow House" at Arles in the south of France in 1888. He painted this room to celebrate his new, settled life. He thought this work, strong and simple, was one of his best paintings, and later he painted two more copies of it.

Glossary

background: the part of a picture or painting that seems to be the farthest from the viewer.

fade: lose color or freshness.

fainter: weaker or dimmer.

foreground: the part of a picture or painting that seems to be the closest to the viewer.

glimpse: see for a brief moment; see a small part of something.

hazy: not clear; blocked from view by fine dust, smoke, or water vapor.

impressionists: painters from the 1870s who believed in painting the first "impression" of their subjects in short dabs of colors, conveying reflected light more than a realistic image.

landscape: a setting of natural scenery.

perspective: the ability to show objects on a flat surface as they appear spatially in real life.

rickety: broken down; about to fall apart.

rout: a major defeat in battle.

soar: rise high into the sky.

Web Sites

Metropolitan Museum of Art Kids Page
www.metmuseum.org/htmlfile/
education/kid.html

Musée d'art Américain Giverny (for kids)
giverny.org/museums/american/
kids/index.htm

Due to the dynamic nature of the Internet, some web sites stay current longer than others. To find additional web sites, use a reliable search engine with one or more of the following keywords: *art, Edgar Degas, Claude Monet, Odyssey, painting,* and *Vincent van Gogh.*

Index